A Self-Love
Workbook and
Guided Journal For
The Amazing Girl
You Are

Building Your Self-Esteem, Overcoming Anxiety, and Learning To Love Yourself

This Workbook Belongs to:

_____

_____

Table of Contents

CHAPTER 1
Introduction

Hi there! My name is Alexis, and I remember all too well what being a teenage girl was all about. Part of my job is helping teens like you who are dealing with issues like stress, anxiety, frustrations, peer pressure, bullying, depression, and confidence struggles. It's normal to feel alone and that no one is struggling like you. But trust me, they are. Some people just hide it better.

Your body and your mind are developing at crazy speeds, and unfortunately, sometimes, all these physical changes can only make the feelings you are having worse. Are you having problems with friends, parents, and teachers? Perhaps you are struggling with body issues, hating your appearance, and feeling awkward. These are all topics this workbook will help you recognize and manage.

This book contains activities, challenges, exercises, and relaxation techniques that are fun and easy to do. You can do them at your own pace and skip around if it suits you best.

However you got this book, whether it be from a parent, teacher, counselor, or just bought it for yourself, I am glad you have it and even happier that I can be a part of your journey to be the best you. Being a teen is hard! But with the right tips and tricks, you can navigate challenging times, feel more confident, have better self-esteem, and learn to love all you are.

-Alexis

You Are Wonderfully Unique and Extraordinary

I designed this workbook for the beautiful, amazing girl you are.

Sometimes you might have good and bad days, and it is hard to remember how special you are.

You might feel upset because of what someone said about you, or you are struggling in school, maybe feeling lonely and worried about what others think about you.

Coming up, you will learn tips and tricks to:

- Improve your self-confidence and self-esteem.
- Overcome anxiety and negative thoughts.
- Manage unwanted bullying and harmful behaviors from others.
- Learn to love yourself and your body.
- Use creative relaxation techniques to improve your mood and stress levels.

You are not alone! I am here to help you achieve your best self and get through these challenging years with confidence and happiness.

Let's get started!

Identify Your Strengths

What are some of your strengths?

1. What are your most unique strengths that no one has?

2. How well do you utilize your strengths daily?

3. What are you proud of?

4. What was the last compliment that you received?

Hidden Strengths

1. List any two hidden strengths that you have no one knows about.

2. Have you tried to develop and master them?

3. What could encourage you to use them more?

Achieving your Goals

Identify your strengths that will help you achieve your goals.

Goal :

Strengthening your goals

Which unique strength would support you in achieving your goal?

How does that help your goal?

What can you do in 5 days to move toward your goal?

Challenging your goal

What stops you from achieving your goal?

How would it impact your goal?

What are your greatest strengths?

CHAPTER 2
I Am Worth It

Who am I Task Cards
These task cards can help you to reflect about yourself.

My top three unique qualities

1.

2.

3.

My three special skills

1.

2.

3.

Who am I Task Cards

These task cards can help you to reflect about yourself.

Three ways you help others

1.

2.

3.

Three things you are proud of

1.

2.

3.

Do More of What You Love

5 things you love to do	5 things you don't like to do
✦	✦
✦	✦
✦	✦
✦	✦
✦	✦

1 Which of your strengths helps you in doing what you love?

2 Do your choices affect your journey toward your dreams?

3 During your bad days, which of your strengths helps you through them?

Postive-Affirmations and Daily Gratitude

Positive affirmations are an important tool to reprogram the negative thoughts about ourselves that like to creep into our minds.

Telling yourself a daily affirmation and envisioning it happening can give us confidence, help us make it come true, and improve our self-esteem.

Positive affirmations help you see yourself positively when you need a confidence boost!

When we love ourselves and feel positive about ourselves, our lives are happier and less stressful, and we are more likely to succeed.

Gratitude helps you stay in a healthy frame of mind longer, be more mindful of positive experiences, improve your mental and physical health and become more optimistic.

You are also in a better mindset to overcome challenges and build solid relationships.

Daily Affirmations

This is an excellent page to tear out and cut into daily affirmations. Place them around your house, your mirror, your computer, your purse, or anywhere else you will frequently see them for a reminder.

I am confident and comfortable in my own skin

I am grateful for my life

I don't need anyone to validate me

I am freaking amazing

I am perfect the way I am

I have a beautiful mind and body

When I want something, I go for it

I don't allow others to bring me down

I am worthy. I am loved. I am enough.

I am resilient and can get through anything

I am beautiful, confident, and smart

I don't need others to make me feel good

DAILY AFFIRMATION AND GRATITUDE JOURNAL

S M T W T F S

DAILY POSITIVE AFFIRMATION	I AM GRATEFUL FOR

SELF-KINDNESSS PLANS FOR TODAY

-
-
-

I AM AMAZING BECAUSE:	TODAY I AM FEELING:

DAILY AFFIRMATION AND GRATITUDE JOURNAL

S M T W T F S

DAILY POSITIVE AFFIRMATION

I AM GRATEFUL FOR

SELF-KINDNESSS PLANS FOR TODAY

-
-
-

I AM AMAZING BECAUSE:

TODAY I AM FEELING:

DAILY AFFIRMATION AND
GRATITUDE JOURNAL

S M T W T F S

DAILY POSITIVE AFFIRMATION

I AM GRATEFUL FOR

SELF-KINDNESSS PLANS FOR TODAY

-
-
-

I AM AMAZING BECAUSE:

TODAY I AM FEELING:

DAILY AFFIRMATION AND
GRATITUDE JOURNAL

(S) (M) (T) (W) (T) (F) (S)

DAILY POSITIVE AFFIRMATION

I AM GRATEFUL FOR

SELF-KINDNESSS PLANS FOR TODAY

-
-
-

I AM AMAZING BECAUSE:

TODAY I AM FEELING:

DAILY AFFIRMATION AND GRATITUDE JOURNAL

S M T W T F S

DAILY POSITIVE AFFIRMATION

I AM GRATEFUL FOR

SELF-KINDNESSS PLANS FOR TODAY

-
-
-

I AM AMAZING BECAUSE:

TODAY I AM FEELING:

DAILY AFFIRMATION AND GRATITUDE JOURNAL

S M T W T F S

DAILY POSITIVE AFFIRMATION

I AM GRATEFUL FOR

SELF-KINDNESSS PLANS FOR TODAY

-
-
-

I AM AMAZING BECAUSE:

TODAY I AM FEELING:

DAILY AFFIRMATION AND GRATITUDE JOURNAL

S M T W T F S

DAILY POSITIVE AFFIRMATION

I AM GRATEFUL FOR

SELF-KINDNESSS PLANS FOR TODAY

-
-
-

I AM AMAZING BECAUSE:

TODAY I AM FEELING:

WORTHINESS WORKSHEET

How do you feel right now?   Date

☆☆☆☆☆   _____

Today I commit to

_____

_____

An affirmation that I promise to keep up to myself today

_____

_____

Today I am proud that

_____

_____

WORTHINESS WORKSHEET

Date

☆☆☆☆☆   _____

Today I commit to

_____

_____

An affirmation that I promise to keep up to myself today

_____

_____

Today I am proud that

_____

_____

Reflection Sheet

Did you achieve your goal?

☐ ☐

Yes

Best part of the day

Things I am grateful for today

Reflection Sheet

Did you achieve your goal?

☐ ☐

Yes

Best part of the day

Things I am grateful for today

CHAPTER 3
Self- Inspection

MIRROR! MIRROR!

Look in a mirror and write seven things that you love about yourself in the mirror below

THINGS IN MY LIFE
I CAN CONTROL

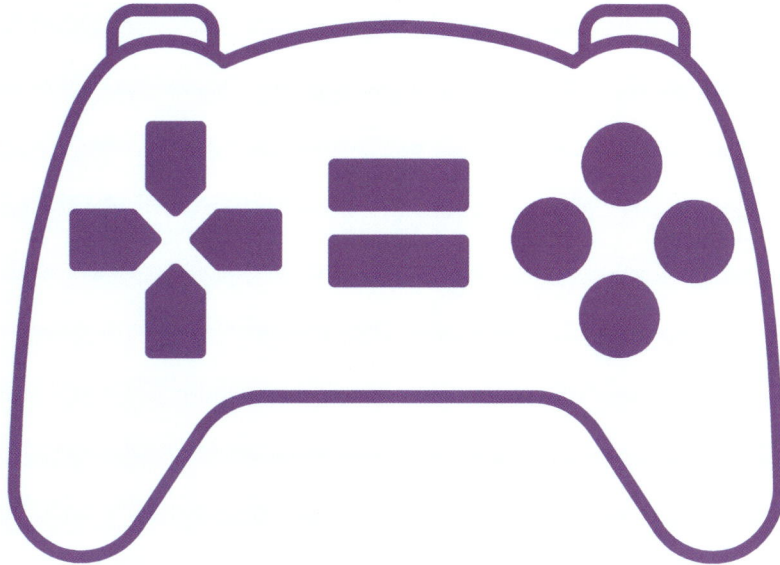

_____ _____

_____ _____

_____ _____

_____ _____

_____ _____

_____ _____

_____ _____

THINGS IN MY LIFE I CANNOT CONTROL

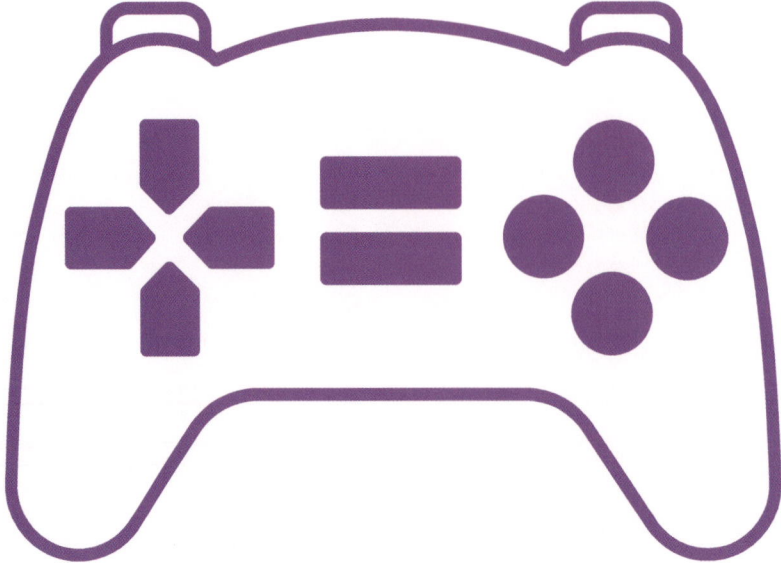

_____   _____

_____   _____

_____   _____

_____   _____

_____   _____

_____   _____

_____   _____

23

DAILY SELF-KINDNESS ACTIONS TO MAKE WHICH JUMP START YOUR SELF-ESTEEM

DELETE ANY APP THAT HURTS YOUR CONFIDENCE AND SELF-ESTEEM

MUTE ANY SOCIAL MEDIA GROUP THAT DISTRACTS YOU TOO MUCH AND CAN BE HURTFUL

DON'T MAKE MULTIPLE TO-DO LISTS IN ONE DAY. AVOID GETTING OVERWHELMED.

SPEND LESS TIME AROUND TOXIC PEOPLE AND ENVIRONMENTS.

DO MORE STRETCHES IN BETWEEN STUDY SESSIONS.

Extra Space for Thoughts

Extra Space for Thoughts

CHAPTER 4
Change Your Outlook

POSITIVE SELF-TALK FLOWER

WRITE A POSITIVE FACT ABOUT YOURSELF IN EACH
PETAL THAT YOU ACCOMPLISHED THIS MONTH

Write a letter to yourself to read one year from now. Describe what your life will look like and what changes you hope you have made.

_____

_____

_____

_____

_____

_____

_____

_____

_____

_____

_____

_____

_____

GRATITUDE JAR

WRITE THINGS THAT YOU ARE GRATEFUL FOR IN YOUR LIFE

Thank You

LET IT GO!

THESE BALLOONS REPRESENT A CHANCE TO GET RID OF NEGATIVE FEELINGS LIKE NAGGING THOUGHTS, WORRIES, ANGER AND SADNESS. WRITE SOME WORDS THAT REPRESENT THOSE FOR YOU AND LET THEM GO!

30

Instead of this...

Use this exercise to work on changing mean negative thoughts you sometimes have into positive, self-esteem, self-love building responses

INSTEAD OF THIS	SAY THIS
I am so dumb, I will fail the test	This test will be hard, but I can do it

RAYS OF POSITIVE SUPPORT

WRITE THE NAMES OF FRIENDS AND FAMILY WHO ARE YOUR SUPPORT SYSTEM

RAYS OF NEGATIVITY AWARENESS

WRITE THE NAMES OF PEOPLE OR ACTIVITIES THAT DON'T BRING YOU JOY AND LOVE

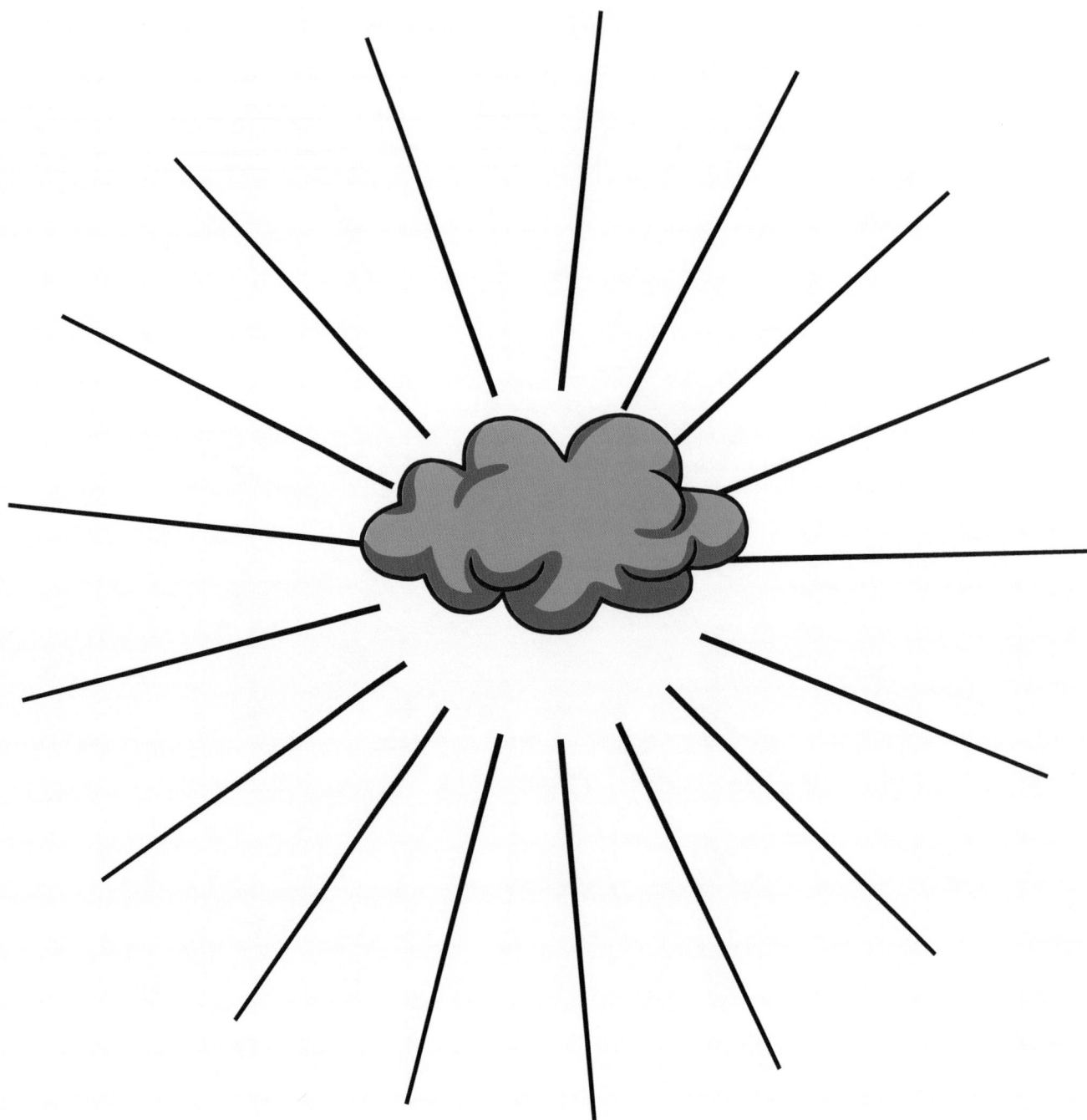

Chapter 5
Self-Esteem to the Rescue!

Self-esteem is how you value and see yourself. It can influence your motivations, life choices, mental well-being, and overall quality of life.

It also has to do with your sense of worthiness or unworthiness.

A negative self-perception can quickly derail you and cause depression, anxiety, low self-confidence, and other health problems.

Key elements to self-esteem include:

- Self-confidence
- Feelings of security
- A strong sense of self
- Sense of belonging
- Feeling of competence

Ways to improve low self-esteem
- Recognize what you're good at.
- Build positive relationships.
- Be kind to yourself.
- Learn to be assertive.
- Start saying "no" without regret.
- Give yourself a new challenge.

Self-Esteem Journal

Date : _____

MON	Something I did well today... Today I had fun when... I felt proud when...
TUE	Today I accomplished... I had a positive experience with... Something I did for someone...
WED	I felt good about myself when... I was proud of someone else... Today was interesting because...
THU	Something I did well today... Today I had fun when... I felt proud when...
FRI	Today I accomplished... I had a positive experience with... Something I did for someone...
SAT	I felt good about myself when... I was proud of someone else... Today was interesting because...
SUN	Something I did well today... Today I had fun when... I felt proud when...

Self-Esteem Journal

Date : _____

MON	Something I learned quickly today... Today I smiled when... I felt strong after...
TUE	Today I finished... I was proud of myself when... Something I did for someone...
WED	I felt good about myself when... I felt positive about myself when... Today was mind opening because...
THU	Something I said that was funny today... Today I had fun when... I felt proud of myself when...
FRI	Today I tried something new... I felt good about myself when.... Something I did for someone felt good...
SAT	I felt good about myself body today when... I was proud of myself after I... Today was challenging because...
SUN	I made a new... I changed my thinking when... I felt proud of myself when...

Self-Esteem Journal

Date : _____

MON	I said something kind when… I acknowledged and accepted a harsh feeling when… I felt proud when…
TUE	I kicked butt today doing… I had a positive experience with… Something I did for someone…
WED	I tried something new.. I stepped up even though I was nervous when… I took a risk when…
THU	I learned this about myself today… Today I tried something scary when… I worked past my worries today by…
FRI	I said something brave when… I had a positive experience with… I took a chance today when..
SAT	I really accomplished this today… I had a positive feeling about my image today when… Today I took time for myself when…
SUN	Today I avoided conflict when… Today I felt great about myself when… I loved myself when…

SELF REFLECTION

THINGS I AM GOOD AT

- _____
- _____
- _____
- _____

COMPLIMENTS I GOT RECENTLY

- _____
- _____
- _____
- _____

WHAT I LIKE ABOUT MY APPEARANCE

- _____
- _____
- _____
- _____

CHALLENGES I HAVE OVERCOME

- _____
- _____
- _____
- _____

I'VE HELPED OTHERS BY

- _____
- _____
- _____
- _____

THINGS THAT ARE UNIQUE ABOUT ME

- _____
- _____
- _____
- _____

I VALLUE THIS THE MOST

- _____
- _____
- _____
- _____

NOTES

SELF REFLECTION

THINGS I AM GOOD AT

- _____
- _____
- _____
- _____

COMPLIMENTS I GOT RECENTLY

- _____
- _____
- _____
- _____

WHAT I LIKE ABOUT MY APPEARANCE

- _____
- _____
- _____
- _____

CHALLENGES I HAVE OVERCOME

- _____
- _____
- _____
- _____

I'VE HELPED OTHERS BY

- _____
- _____
- _____
- _____

THINGS THAT ARE UNIQUE ABOUT ME

- _____
- _____
- _____
- _____

I VALLUE THIS THE MOST

- _____
- _____
- _____
- _____

NOTES

SELF REFLECTION

THINGS I AM GOOD AT

- _____
- _____
- _____
- _____

COMPLIMENTS I GOT RECENTLY

- _____
- _____
- _____
- _____

WHAT I LIKE ABOUT MY APPEARANCE

- _____
- _____
- _____
- _____

CHALLENGES I HAVE OVERCOME

- _____
- _____
- _____
- _____

I'VE HELPED OTHERS BY

- _____
- _____
- _____
- _____

THINGS THAT ARE UNIQUE ABOUT ME

- _____
- _____
- _____
- _____

I VALLUE THIS THE MOST

- _____
- _____
- _____
- _____

NOTES

Journaling Starters

I feel good when	I feel proud when	I am the happiest when
I feel strong when	People are kind to me when	My best accomplishment
My biggest support system is	One thing I love about my life	I am really good at

Extra Prompts

_____

_____

MY DO'S AND DON'T LISTS

DATE:

TODAY'S AFFIRMATION

I'M THANKFUL FOR

① _____
② _____
③ _____
④ _____

TODAY'S GOALS

① _____
② _____
③ _____

TOP PRIORITIES

① _____
② _____
③ _____

OBSTACLES THAT MAY OCCUR

_____

_____

_____

MUST NOT DO

○ _____
○ _____
○ _____
○ _____
○ _____
○ _____
○ _____
○ _____
○ _____
○ _____
○ _____
○ _____
○ _____
○ _____
○ _____
○ _____
○ _____
○ _____
○ _____
○ _____
○ _____
○ _____
○ _____
○ _____
○ _____

WATER

TOMORROW'S GOALS

① _____
② _____
③ _____

MY DO'S AND DON'T LISTS

DATE:

TODAY'S AFFIRMATION

_____

I'M THANKFUL FOR

1. _____
2. _____
3. _____
4. _____

TODAY'S GOALS

1. _____
2. _____
3. _____

TOP PRIORITIES

1. _____
2. _____
3. _____

OBSTACLES THAT MAY OCCUR

_____

_____

_____

MUST NOT DO

- ○ _____
- ○ _____
- ○ _____
- ○ _____
- ○ _____
- ○ _____
- ○ _____
- ○ _____
- ○ _____
- ○ _____
- ○ _____
- ○ _____
- ○ _____
- ○ _____
- ○ _____
- ○ _____
- ○ _____
- ○ _____
- ○ _____
- ○ _____
- ○ _____
- ○ _____
- ○ _____
- ○ _____
- ○ _____
- ○ _____

WATER

TOMORROW'S GOALS

1. _____
2. _____
3. _____

43

CHAPTER 6
Love Your Body

Body Positivity Journal

Special activities for you to celebrate your perfectly unique and beautiful body

What is Body Positivity?

IS IT A STATE OF MIND?

Body positivity is the belief that everyone deserves to feel good about themselves, regardless of what social media and popular culture consider to be the ideal size, shape, look, and dress..

Body positivity also influences how teens feel about their bodies, including how they perceive food, exercise, weight, sexual health, and self-care.

Why is Body Positivity Such a Struggle Sometimes?

When teens have a positive view of their appearance and bodies they are more confident, happier, and healthier.

Those who have a negative view of their bodies are more likely to develop eating disorders and despair.

So what can you do to keep a positive body image when you are bombarded with images of "perfect bodies" on social media and television?

Although the goal of body positivity is to promote acceptance and appreciation of your body, it can be difficult since it adds yet another layer of pressure and crazy expectations.

46

How Do I Maintain Body Positivity?
Practical Tips and Advice

1 Adopt body Neutrality

2 Be active

3 Practice Focused Self Care

4 Avoid comparing yourself

5 Join body positive communities

6 Ask for help

7 Take a break

8 Do something you're good at

9 Accept who you are

10 Care for others

EMBRACE YOUR FLAWS!

Some of us are funny, some of us are mathematicians, and some of us can cook. We are all unique. Accepting your individuality is considerably healthier than wishing you were more like someone else. A positive self-image gives you more confidence to pick up new talents, explore new locations, and meet new people. Self-confidence makes it easier for you to handle challenging situations in life.

Be proud of who you are!! Recognize and accept the things you may not be good at, and focus on what you can do well. There are many more of those.

If there's anything about yourself you would like to change, are your expectations realistic? If they are, work towards the change in small steps. Don't wish you were 6ft tall, you can only control so much.

I appreciate being present in the moment because I am content with who I am.

49

SELF REMINDER

You be you, you do you!

Don't let others' opinions dictate your life.

Try every day to stand up to that urge to change yourself and "fit in."

50

Body Positivity Journal

List healthy tasks to think about and accomplish each day.
Below are some prompts to get you started. Check them off
when you've completed them.

- [ ] Who has inspired me when it comes to loving myself?
- [ ] What are ten things I love about my body today?
- [ ] What is one thing I can do today to better appreciate my body?
- [ ] Where do I feel stuck and what do I need to let go of in order to grow?
- [ ] How do I define beauty and what does it mean for me?
- [ ]
- [ ]
- [ ]
- [ ]
- [ ]
- [ ]
- [ ]
- [ ]
- [ ]
- [ ]
- [ ]
- [ ]
- [ ]
- [ ]

CHAPTER 7
BULLYING AND OTHER UNWANTED BEHAVIORS

How to Cope with Bullying and Other Negative, Hurtful Behaviors

What is Bullying?

Bullying is a form of aggressive behavior in which someone intentionally causes physical and emotional injury to another person through unwanted words or actions. It is a way to seek power over another person and is a severe form of aggression that isn't always physical.

More people are bullied through emotional and verbal abuse, which can occur in person, through others, and, more frequently, online via texts and posts.

- Cyberbullying is verbally threatening or harassing behavior conducted through electronic technology, such as emails, social media, or text messaging. Cyber Bullying can be even more painful for the victim as they have no control over the internet, and when something is online, it is there forever.

The bullied victim typically has trouble defending themselves and has difficulty stopping what is happening to them. They have done absolutely nothing to "cause" the bullying, and it often leads to feelings of fearfulness, depression, stress, and anxiety; in extreme circumstances, it can lead to feelings of hopelessness and suicidal thoughts.

Asking parents, friends, teachers, and counselors can often embarrass, intimidate, and be worrisome for the victim. Sometimes they might feel weak, scared, or concerned it will cause the bullying to be even worse.

There are ways to manage this, I promise you. It isn't a one time-fix, but you can get through this. Building courage and confidence and reaching out for help are all actions you can learn to do with support. Staying "STOP IT" can feel impossible, but you can learn how to do it and feel proud of yourself.

Identifying Bullying

Do any of these apply to you?

1. Someone threatening you. ☐

2. Teasing you. ☐

3. Posting an embarrassing photo of you. ☐

4. Telling others not to talk to you. ☐

5. Spreading rumors about you. ☐

6. Revealing private information in public. ☐

7. Leaving you out on purpose. ☐

STEPS TO STOPPING A BULLY
IN THE MOMENT

BELOW ARE STEPS YOU CAN TRY WHICH TAKE A BULLY'S POWER AWAY. IF YOU ARE NOT READY TO TRY THESE, LOOK TO A SUPPORTIVE, SAFE SOURCE TO HELP YOU. YOU DON'T HAVE TO FACE THIS ALONE.

01 If you can, stand up straight and say "STOP DOING..." (insert action)

02 Hold your hand out and say 'ENOUGH.' Show that you will stand up for yourself and not accept such hurtful actions.

03 Look them in the eye, show your quiet confidence, and walk away to a safe area. Sometimes silence can be a decisive action.

04 Find out your safe source and ask for advice or help. Maybe a friend, favorite teacher, family member, neighbor, church leader, or online resource. Asking for help empowers YOU and takes the bully's control away.

05 If you are physically, emotionally, or cyber-bullied, talk to a support source and plan how to handle this IMMEDIATELY. Love yourself and take your power back.

You are Stronger Than You Think

Being victimized by cruel, unwanted behavior is never something to ignore, and hope goes away. Even one incident of cruelty by another can cause significant damage to your self-esteem and confidence.

Strangely, those who seek to hurt others will often have significant confidence issues themselves. What will make you emotionally stronger is taking charge of this negative situation. Whether it is just one cruel text, one gossipy story about you, or a pattern of behavior that causes you to feel depressed and embarrassed, you can end this and come out with even more self-confidence and.. self-esteem.

Asking people you trust for help is essential. You don't have to feel alone.

CHAPTER 8

STRESS MANAGEMENT

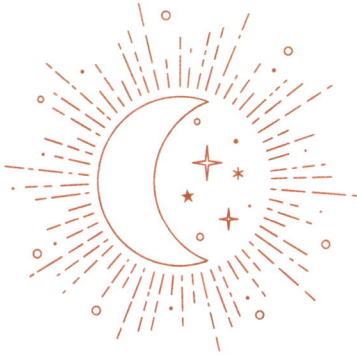

THOUGHT AWARENESS

Think about a stressful situation in your life right now. What stressful, negative words, feelings, and sensations come to mind? Just write them all down as they come to you. There doesn't have to be any order. An example might be: "I feel sad sometimes."

Negative Thoughts

The next step is to take those words and create an opposite, rational thought. Turn "I feel sad" into: " I feel sad, but I just need to figure out why?" Look at every word you wrote, and what solves the worry? What would you advise someone else?

Rational Thoughts

Now take the exact words, both negative and rational, and come up with a positive thought. "It's normal to feel sad sometimes. But I can control how long I choose to be sad and do things that make me happy."

Positive Thoughts

RE-TRAIN OUR BRAINS

Reducing Stress by Changing Your Thinking

Understand that we create negative thought patterns, which become automatic habits. For example, whenever you look in the mirror, you think, "I look bad." It is essential to understand what started the negative thoughts.

Step 1: Identify the Situation

Describe the situation that triggered your negative mood.

Step 2: Analyze Your Mood

Describe how you felt in the situation, and how you're feeling now.

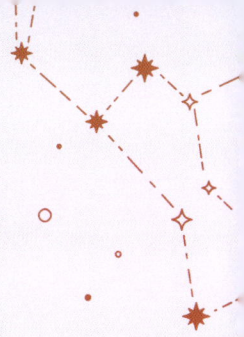

Step 3: Identify Automatic Thoughts

Make a list of your first negative thoughts that sometimes pop in your mind.

Step 4: What are positive alternatives you could have said?

Write anything down the opposite of these negative thoughts.

Step 5: Monitor Your Present Mood

Now take a second and think about your mood after coming up with a better, healthier thought pattern. How does that make you feel>

Understanding
YOUR PROBLEMS

Try to take a hard situation right now and process it from start to finish with what you want to happen. Look for old patterns that might keep you stuck. What is a new way you can handle it?

Situation

Feelings

Thoughts

Physical Symptoms

Behaviors

COPING ASSESSMENT SCALE

Mark how often you use each of these coping strategies in your day-to-day life.

	Always	Rarely	Never
Use my words to hurt others	☐	☐	☐
Physically harm others	☐	☐	☐
Take 'time out' when I am low	☐	☐	☐
Yell at others	☐	☐	☐
Do deep breathing	☐	☐	☐
Make threats	☐	☐	☐
Talk to a friend about my feelings	☐	☐	☐
Tell my teachers or parents	☐	☐	☐
Name call other people	☐	☐	☐
Hurt myself	☐	☐	☐

Relax
with
Coloring

Research has consistently shown that coloring helps improve out mental and emotional states.

While reducing stress and anxiety, it also stabilizes emotions through meditative, relaxing creation.

When you need a mental break, put away technology and pull out your colored pencils, crayons, markers or paints, and sit in a quiet place and enjoy the next few pages.

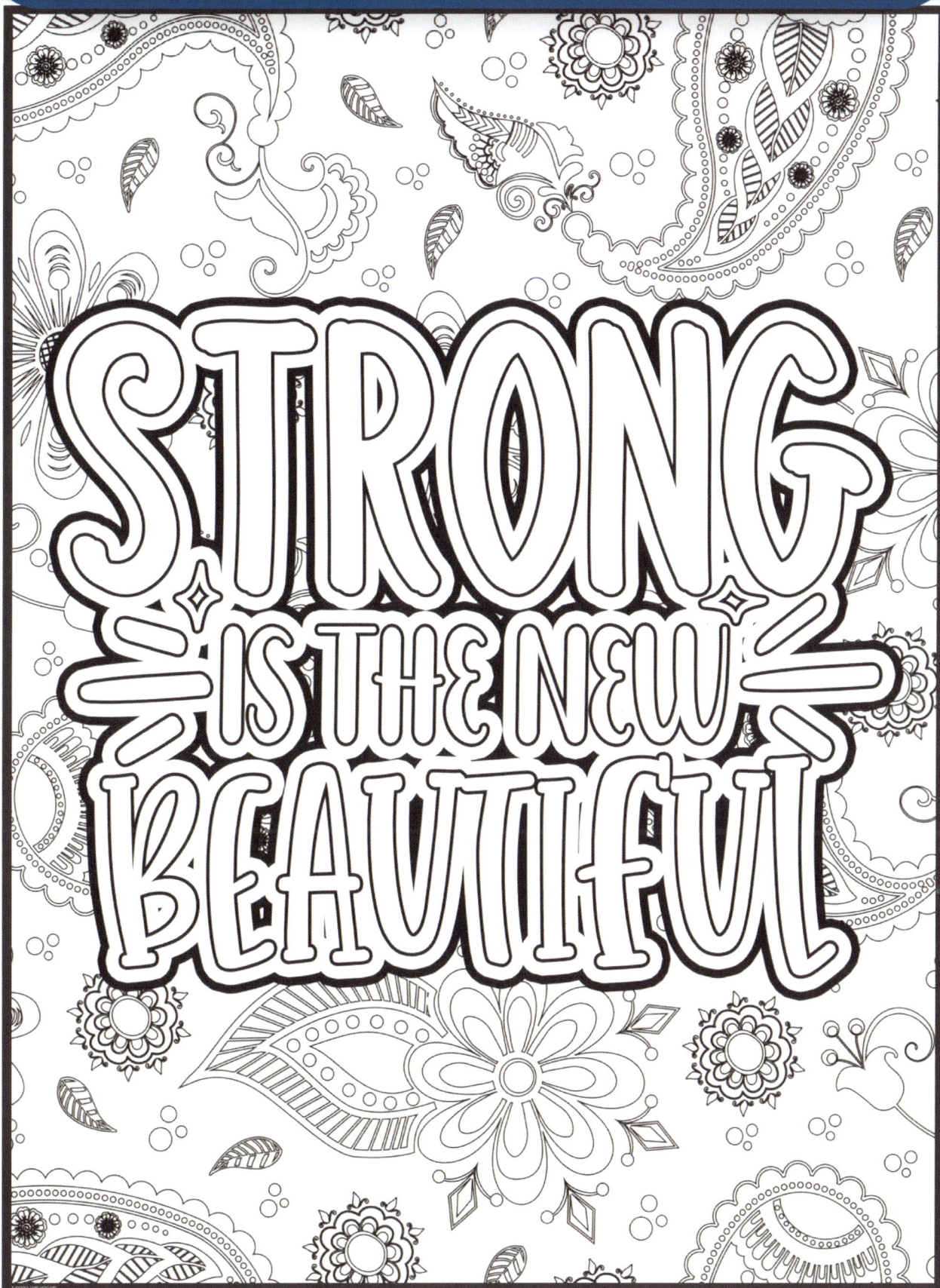

STRONG IS THE NEW BEAUTIFUL

YOU CAN DO ANYTHING YOU SET YOUR MIND TO

BE
STRONGER
THAN
Your
EXCUSES

LIFE LAUGH LOVE

81

Additional Resources

If you would like to find out more about the coloring book pages that were included, please refer to the following titles by Alexis Carter on Amazon:

- *Relax with Motivational Quotes Coloring Book for Girls*

- *Relax with Flowers, A Coloring Book for Adults*

- *Relax with Animals, A Coloring Book for Adults*

- *Relax with Mindfulness Meditations, A Coloring Book for Adults*

Scan Below for Amazon Links

ABOUT THE AUTHOR

Alexis Carter has a master's degree and a specialty in behavioral psychology. She has expertise in developing self-awareness, coping strategies, and recognizing negative patterns and self-esteem issues, which can be translated into personal lives, relationships, and work environments.

Alexis's goal is to arm teens, women, and men with practical strategies and coping techniques to achieve personal success, understand ingrained behavioral patterns and manage challenges affecting self-development and goals. She has created a library of over 20 books, workbooks, self-help titles, and adult coloring books designed to address self-esteem, confidence building, stress management, and developing mindfulness.

Alexis is a working mom of twins and lives in California with her children.

My Thanks

Dear Reader,

Thank you for giving yourself time and completing this self-love workbook and journal. I am passionate about helping teens achieve their best and truly enjoyed creating this workbook for you.

Many readers do not know how critical reviews are for an author and how difficult they are to come by.

I would be very grateful if you could write a brief review on Amazon. If you have suggestions for improvement or additional content, don't hesitate to get in touch with me directly at:
www.creativeworksbooks.com.

Thank you for sharing your thoughts, and I wish you all the best in your self-improvement journey.

Alexis